How To Manage Your Money

How To Make Money, As Well As Your Current Financial
Situation: How To Successfully Regulate And Manage
Your Current Financial Situation

*(Increasing Your Savings, Eliminating Your Debt, And
Establishing Your Financial Security)*

SiegmarHagemann

TABLE OF CONTENT

How To Save Money

It's always a good idea to save Money! Recognize why? While it is true that you cannot buy everything, Money can help you get most things. This brief sentence captures the importance of saving Money. But let's read on for a deeper understanding of the same.

What Does Saving Money Mean?

The following five definitions should aid in our understanding of what it means to save Money:

A Brief Explanation of Savings: Saving money is reserving a portion of your regular income for unexpected expenses. Furthermore, saved or saved Money is the sum of Money that remains after covering essential and base costs.

To Put Away a Small Amount of Money to Cover Future Needs - Another way to think of saving Money is as a method that entails reserving a tiny amount of your income for unforeseen future costs.

Saving Money Requires Smart Money Management: Learning how to save Money helps you understand how important it is to make informed financial decisions. Not only can saving help you manage your finances well, but it also comes in helpful when things are tight. Therefore, saving Money is often referred to as a process that teaches you how to use Money wisely because it involves finding the right balance between your savings and expenditures.

According to another definition, saving Money creates sufficient planning for future requirements. It also refers to "to set aside a particular amount of money for future expenses"! It is up to you to decide whether to use your resources for current needs or to put them aside for future expenses.

Saving Money Leads to a Better Life - The culmination of the concepts above states that the first step to a happier and better life is conserving Money! It entails managing your finances sensibly to set aside a small portion of your income for short- or long-term needs.

Why is creating a financial budget so important?

We kindly request that you read the following arguments to convince you of the benefits of saving Money instead of consuming anything you earn.

Makes Your Life Happier and Better When your financial situation is stable, you stay at ease and worry-free. Saving Money is the key to having financial security. You always feel satisfied and at rest when you have Money in your savings account since you know you can take it out and spend it anytime you need to. The savings can be prudently applied to various expenses, such as home loan payments, health insurance, or other expenses, opening the door to a more fulfilling and happy life! Meets needs for the future as well as the present. You never know when you could require cash!

Whether for an enticing deal or an urgent medical crisis, you need money. Money to satisfy your desires! You can never fail at saving Money. Rather, it gives you the freedom to spend Money as you like.

Helps You Make Money During Inflation: You can frequently invest your savings and use them for savings. Your saved Money could be invested in gold, real estate, bank scams, and other lucrative plans and schemes. These investments are quite beneficial when inflation is present. When prices rise due to the higher rates, the value of your assets increases. Thus, if you sell at the right time, you might profit!

Enhances the probability that financial objectives will be met – No financial goal can be met without cash! Additionally, you must have access to Money when needed if you hope to accomplish any financial goal within a specific time frame. It's important to remember that if you maintain a financial objective, you should also maintain the funds! Deducting Money from your current paycheck is the simplest way to accomplish this.

Greetings for a Wealthy Retirement - The years following your retirement could be the most enjoyable and exciting of your life if you have enough Money in your account to meet various costs. Using the savings previously invested in successful plans that remain ripe throughout your retirement era is the easiest approach to enjoying retirement. If you invest your saved Money in quality health plans, insurance, etc., you won't have to worry about anything when you're retired. The most important thing is that you will not be dependent on anyone.

Guards Against Currency Fluctuation: One never knows when currency fluctuations will occur. Saving Money regularly is the best way to avoid being vulnerable during difficult economic times. You can use the saved Money as needed.

Since future increases are anticipated in daily general expenses, saving Money is always beneficial. Your regular expenses grow over time, Whether for normal foods, building supplies, or household products. For example, you and your partner recently tied the knot and will shortly have a child. Your child will start school in a few years, and then, in still more years, he or she will pursue further education. Due to the constant life changes, so are our costs. Every day costs are increasing! Thus, saving Money for future needs is a wise decision.

Advantages of Giving Your Kids Financial and Educational Support: Your kids look to you for all of their financial needs, for additional schooling, getting into a respectable school, or anything else. You can better meet your children's financial and educational needs by reserving a portion of your salary regularly.

Outstanding financial and social standing People who save Money at the right time don't require financial help from others. Furthermore, the Money you save adds up rapidly to a sizeable amount you can invest.

These investments and wise financial decisions can help you attain a respectable financial and social standing in society.

Escape Spontaneous Expenditure: As soon as you start saving and building wealth, you prevent yourself from ever being a spendthrift. You stop wasting Money or making needless purchases.

Sometimes, the most difficult thing is just to start saving. You can save for all your short- and long-term goals by using this step-by-step guide to help you create a simple and realistic strategy.

Monitor your expenses.

To start saving Money:

Figure out how much you now spend.

Keep track of every penny you spend, including regular monthly instalments and purchases of household goods like coffee and groceries.

Record your expenses however it is most comfortable for you, whether using a pen and paper, an app, a basic spreadsheet, or a free online spending tracker.

Once you have your data, total each sum by grouping the figures into food, gasoline, and mortgage categories.

Check your credit card and bank statements to be sure you have everything.

Make Savings A Priority In Your Budget.

Now that you know how much you spend each month, you can create a budget. Your budget should show you how your expenses and income are related so that you can keep track of your spending and avoid going overboard.

Be sure to include expenses such as regular car maintenance, even though they don't occur every month. Incorporate a savings section into your budget, and initially aim to save as much as feels manageable. Ultimately, you want to save 15–20% of your salary.

Successful investors' and entrepreneurs' mindsets and habits

A common mindset and behaviours among prosperous investors and entrepreneurs have enabled them to accomplish their objectives and amass riches. The following are some essential mentalities and practices of prosperous businesspeople and investors:

Vision: Successful investors and entrepreneurs create quantifiable, precise targets to realize their vision for the future. They set goals and pursue them with determination and well-thought-out approaches.

Risk-taking: As failure is an inevitable part of the process, successful businesspeople and investors don't hesitate to take chances. They take lessons from their mistakes and turn them into chances to improve.

Creativity and innovation: Prosperous investors and entrepreneurs are frequently very creative and innovative people who are always looking for new ventures and chances to expand.

Flexibility and adaptability: Successful businesspeople and investors can modify their plans and tactics in response to changing conditions. They have the flexibility to quickly adjust to changing market conditions, fresh opportunities, and unforeseen difficulties.

The ability to assess data and information, spot trends and patterns, and make well-informed judgments that advance their objectives are all characteristics of successful investors and entrepreneurs.

Perpetual education and personal development: Prosperous businesspeople and financiers are ever-evolving individuals who consistently strive to enhance their abilities and comprehension. They are dedicated to their development and professional and personal advancement.

Focus and discipline: Well-achieved business owners and investors possess a strong sense of focus and discipline, enabling them to allocate their time and resources to the things that will help them get closer to their objectives. They stay focused and have a strong sense of direction, avoiding distractions.

Certain mentalities and behaviours that have helped them succeed are common among prosperous investors and business owners. You can improve your chances of reaching your objectives and accumulating riches by developing these qualities and behaviours in yourself.

Exercises and useful advice for developing a success-oriented mindset.

A success-oriented mindset must be deliberately developed through practice and effort. The following useful advice and activities can assist you in cultivating a success-oriented mindset:

Writing in a gratitude journal: Set aside time daily to list your blessings. This can help you develop a positive mindset by refocusing your attention from what you need to what you already have.

Visualization: Envision yourself accomplishing your objectives and leading the life of your dreams. Envision the specifics of your goal and the sensation you will have upon accomplishing it. This might support your motivation and goal-focused persistence.

Positive affirmations: Make a list and tell yourself these daily statements. "I am worthy of success" and "I am capable of achieving my goals" are two examples of positive affirmations.

Dissect your objectives: Break things down into manageable steps and acknowledge your accomplishments. This can support your motivation and momentum as you work toward your bigger objectives.

Take good care of your physical and mental well-being by engaging in self-care. Exercise, a balanced diet, meditation, and quality time with loved ones are some examples. Emotionally and physically well, you'll be more capable of overcoming obstacles and achieving your objectives.

Embrace the beneficial impacts in your environment: Spend time with those that inspire and support you. Look for mentors and role models who have succeeded in fields related to your interests. You can draw inspiration from their viewpoints and experiences and learn from their mistakes and accomplishments.

Concentrate on finding answers: When faced with obstacles, try not to focus on the issue but on seeking solutions. This can support your continued empowerment and proactivity in the face of difficulty.

Celebrate and express gratitude: Honor your accomplishments, no matter how modest. Spend some time reflecting on your achievements and expressing your thanks for the chances that brought you this far.

Developing a success-oriented attitude is an ongoing process that calls for work and repetition. You may cultivate an optimistic and powerful mindset that will support you in reaching your objectives and accumulating riches by putting these useful advice and activities into practice.

2. Not Every Investor Fits Into One Size

Despite how much you all want investors to offer seminars and courses, there are no ways to invest. As John Bogle of Vanguard Investment Fame says, "The key is no secrets."

Profitable investments can be achieved through various methods, as can learning the specifics. Nothing is new under the sun, and no marketer is teaching a specific investing method.

If you don't want to shell out thousands of dollars for a boot camp or lecture by an expensive guru, you might obtain similar content for less than a hundred dollars at your local or online library.

Determining which of the numerous possible investment techniques would be appropriate for your circumstances is the secret to financial stability and one you cannot obtain from the literature or the majority of gurus.

Your investment advice is general; you need it to be tailored. While there is a solution for everyone, not every investment approach is perfect.

It is your responsibility to locate it to get financial stability.

You are a special individual because of your abilities, upbringing, experiences, and views on life. You perceive risks differently than everyone else and have distinct priorities, deadlines, and goals.

How likely is it that you'll attend an investment boot camp or weekend seminar where a specific investment strategy will be tailored to your unique needs? This is not logical.

Most investor education is based on the fallacious notion that "one size fits all."

It has nothing to do with ties, shoes, or sunglasses or involves investing strategies. Not everyone fits into a single size.

Each person has a special gift to offer the world, and an investment strategy that capitalizes on this gift is what leads to financial success. Your early and wealthy retirement will not be like anyone you converse with or hang out with.

It makes it harder for investment seminars, prepackaged advice, and standardized machine solutions to find your facts and test the established "facts" of finance.

The second justification for the significance of financial education is that, as we cover in our extensive wealth-building course, you can design a wealth-creation strategy specific to your abilities, values, and available resources by learning more about the many investing strategies and yourself.

If you don't teach yourself to do so, no one else will.

How To Get Rid Of Conflicts Of Interest In Advisory Investments

The only person who is completely committed to your finances is you. Everyone else is disputing their interest.

Tom Ferry also discussed the importance of financial literacy among Americans and the necessity for improved financial education for students.

"Financial literacy will help deter young people from making bad financial decisions and take years to get through."

No one is as concerned about investing as you are, and you must be knowledgeable about it.

You are the only one in your life who makes financial decisions without conflicts of interest. You are the only other investment expert who appears to be interested in your portfolio.

Everyone is acting in their own best interests.

The third reason financial education is necessary to prevent conflicts of interest is the ability to distinguish between investing in fact and fiction.

4. It Is Possible to Transfer Authority, But Not Responsibility

Most individuals want to think that their advisors are considering important financial issues, including estate planning, insurance, and college funds.

Send the problems to a qualified advisor; don't try to educate yourself. It's going to be handled by you.

You are still accountable for the outcomes of your investments, whether you hire someone or make your investments. You are accountable for the decision you make, which is the choice.

You choose which investment to buy and which investment professional to hire. If you are unhappy with the returns on your investments, you alone are at fault.

Furthermore, you cannot outsource responsibility if you delegate power.

You can always choose wisely when investing if you know what works, what doesn't, and why.

What factors, if not intelligence, are you considering while making investment decisions? Is it the speaker's beauty, the seller's charm, media noises, blind faith, or trust? None of them is a surefire recipe for successful investing.

An intelligence substitute does not exist.

You owe it to your financial future to do otherwise, but you choose not to act by developing the knowledge necessary to make prudent investment choices. Anything less than that is careless.

Your financial education should centre on whether you can manage your finances independently. This brings us to our fourth justification for requiring financial education.

The Advantages of Making Wise Decisions

1. Enhanced Clarity - Illuminating Your Path: Making wise decisions gives you direction clarity. It's similar to turning on a flashlight in a

pitch-black room to show the path forward in the face of uncertainty.

2. Decreased Stress - Lessening the Mental Burden: You're less likely to second-guess or worry about the results when you make well-informed selections. As a result, there is less stress and more mental calm.

3. Empowerment: The Booster of Self-Belief: It gives you the power to make decisions. It gives you more self-assurance and empowers you to take charge of your life.

4. Better Problem Solving - The Adaptability Skill: Effective decision makers hone their problem-solving abilities. They are skilled at situation analysis, developing creative ideas, and making adjustments when things change.

5. Stronger Relationships - Establishing Trust and Respect: You can build trust and respect with people by making deliberate decisions that show you are dependable and considerate.

6. Reaching Objectives - Converting Dreams into Actuality: Making wise decisions helps you get closer to your objectives. Every decision you make aligns with your goals, paving the way for steady advancement.

7. Personal Development - Handling Difficulties: Making decisions is a path of self-awareness and development. Even if your decisions bring obstacles, they also present chances for growth, learning, and adaptation.

Making decisions is what keeps you afloat in the maze of life. You can use it to take advantage of opportunities, overcome obstacles, and control your future. Effective decision-making is your compass when choosing a college, advancing in your job, or allocating your leisure time. Accept this chapter as a toolkit for developing self-awareness, self-assurance, and the capacity to design a life that reflects your goals and desires.

ACTIVITIES

Exercise 1: The Tree of Decisions

This exercise increases your ability to see a choice's various possibilities and outcomes.

1. Sketch a two-branched tree.

Two branches should be labelled "Do it" and "Don't do it."

3. List the various ways your choice could turn out under each branch.

4. Consider the advantages and disadvantages of each result.

5. Select the option you believe will work best for you.

An anecdote to aid in understanding: A teenager is debating whether to study at home or attend a party. He sketches two branches on a decision tree: "Go to the party" and "Stay home and study." He lists the potential results under each branch. He might meet new people and have fun if he attends the party but also run into problems. He might do well on his test if he stays home and studies, but he might also lose out on the party's pleasure. The child believes that staying at home to study is the best course of action for him.

Adopt a boss-like perspective and cultivate the proper mindset. To.

We ought to look at a few more differences.

Monday Mindset

• Workers fear Monday. (Alternatively, however, the day on which their work week begins.)

• Business owners don't just jump into a workweek. They look forward to each day as a new chance to live their dreams.

That's not how I think.

• Workers view everything at work through whether it concerns them.

• Since they are responsible for everything that happens in their business, entrepreneurs view everything as their obligation.

T. G. I. F. (It's Friday, thank God) attitude: Workers always look forward to their days off.

Whether they are "working" or not, entrepreneurs always think about ways to grow their businesses and innovative abilities. They look forward to it every day!

When will my pay increase occur? Attitude: Workers feel that promotions must be given according to a schedule rather than based on their performance.

• Entrepreneurs only occasionally consider when they will receive a raise. They are aware that their prize will be more noticeable the harder they work to improve the lives of others.

Oh my goodness, this current mindset

• Workers approach meetings with a "goodness" mentality.

• Entrepreneurs approach meetings with an inventive attitude. They know that great ideas come out of these get-togethers. We could examine a lot more mindsets than just these. Practically speaking, maintain contact with the pair if, as you read this, they have reminded you of someone.

Creating Wealth

Increasing your net worth through regular action and wise financial decisions is a long-term process that goes into building wealth. We'll talk about methods for gradually accumulating wealth in this chapter.

Creating a Wealthy Attitude

Developing a wealth mindset is the first step towards accumulating wealth. This entails having confidence in your ability to build wealth and being prepared to take chances and give up things to reach your financial objectives. It also entails putting more of an emphasis on long-term financial planning than on quick profits.

Establishing Budgetary Objectives

Establishing clear financial objectives is essential for accumulating wealth. This could be paying off debt, putting money aside for a down payment on a home, or making retirement investments. Make sure your objectives are feasible and reasonable, and divide them into more digestible chunks.

Making a Spending Plan

Creating a budget is a crucial part of becoming wealthy. You can use it to keep tabs on your earnings and outlays, find places to make savings and set aside money for your financial objectives. Make sure your budget accounts for consistent savings contributions.

Investing with Long-Term Views

A crucial element of gradually accumulating wealth is investing. Historically, the stock market has yielded greater returns than bonds or savings accounts, but it carries a bigger risk. A varied portfolio of stocks, bonds, and other assets that match your financial objectives and risk tolerance should be considered when investing. Recall to hold onto your investments for the long run and refrain from acting on impulse in response to transient market swings.

Possession of Real Estate

Over time, accumulating money through real estate ownership can be very effective. Real estate can increase in value over time and generate passive income through rental units. If you want to accumulate equity over time, consider buying a primary property or investing in rental properties.

Establishing a Business

Creating a side business or enterprise is another strategy to gradually accumulate riches. You can make money and acquire a valuable asset by developing a good or service that fills a market demand. Along with dedication and risk-taking, starting a firm requires a willingness to adapt and learn.

7. Saving money is the most crucial stage because it's the only way to completely erase debt!

Since you have to save enough money to handle these financial problems on your own without the assistance of others, you should logically base your borrowing from others on your own needs. We will go into more detail on this topic in the upcoming chapters. These actions are crucial for anyone hoping to stay out of irresponsible debt, which leaves its bearer with nothing but stress and endless issues before starting over from scratch.

WHAT MAY IMPROVE THE PROCESS OF REPAYMENT

Seven financial blunders that make the payback procedure seem impossible:

Additionally, it's not uncommon to make financial errors that inadvertently make debt repayment more difficult.

1. Debts can put you in jail if they are not managed, so readers, don't downplay how serious they are!

The individual could be blind to the potential dangers and losses connected to the debt. His financial perspective is thus limited since he only considers the money he already has and keeps borrowing when things get harder while ignoring the reality that his debt is getting heavier.

2. failing to assess the financial circumstances. Need to be aware of your financial situation!

Debt is not always the best option, so you must consider a few things before deciding. For example, do you need debt right now? Is there a timeframe you can wait until you get enough money? Are there any options available besides debt? These tips assist you in avoiding expensive loans and only using them when necessary.

3. Non-regulation of installment payment schemes

Some people assume that the simplest method to eliminate several monthly instalments is to divide the salary portion of the debt payback over all the instalments. However, this ignores that each installment has a different interest rate and late charge.

4. erroneously calculated expense, preserve it in your wallet.

It's a good idea to create a budget at the start of every month and accurately predict your expenses. Some people overestimate their costs or lose control of spending due to incentives like deals or discounts.

5. I forget when the instalments are due. Yes, it may appear absurd, but there are a lot of issues with it.

Certain debts are not automatically subtracted from your monthly salary when you receive them because the instalment payment deadline may fall in the middle of the month or after you receive your pay for a while. As a result, time can pass, and you may forget the instalment payment deadline, which could result in late fees or fines.

6. Think of indulgences as necessities. You should refrain from doing this because doing so will make you curse yourself!

I know individuals who lead this affluent lifestyle despite debts and a tight budget! Naturally, this made them "badass" financial experts—minus the "bad" bit. Before spending money on luxuries you can live without, you must first pay off the debt instalments. Failure to do so will lessen your chances of paying off the debt quickly.

7. not making the appropriate financial decision. Use your time wisely when conducting your study; you have endless time.

Some people want to invest more money to boost their income, but they make poor or unplanned investments that prevent them from paying off their debt. For instance, a person invests a particular amount to get a 2% profit rate, but 10% is deducted from their account. In this instance, the investments are more detrimental than helpful.

Ensure Yourself Is Better Taken Care Of

P

For me, paying medical bills is akin to having my teeth extracted. (Don't even get me started on paying for genuine tooth extractions.)

I am appreciative of my amazing medical team, but I'll do whatever it takes to avoid having to pay for unnecessary treatment. That may sound ridiculous, but to be perfectly honest, that is one of my key reasons for exercising. Make every effort to look after yourself if you want to lower your cost of living. Consume healthfully. Work out at least a couple of times a week. And after using the loo, wash your damn hands!

5.

Take A Financial Diet

H

To what extent has the statement "I want to lose 15 pounds before summer" been made by you or someone you know? Given the circumstances, how frequently have you heard someone declare, "I want to cut my expenses by $200 per month by the next quarter"?

The latter is far less typical. But one of the best ways to lower your cost of living is to go on a financial diet.

See, there's no difference between a financial and physical diet. All you have to do is create a budget and stick to it for some time. Put differently, you strive to reduce unnecessary expenses in your life.

One advantage of implementing a financial diet is that it doesn't involve abruptly altering your system. Instead, you want to lower your costs over an extended length of time. A financial diet teaches you to make wiser decisions and develop sound financial habits, much like learning to avoid bad meals and go to the gym daily.

Six

Understand The Distinction Between Needs And Wants

O

One of my biggest annoyances is when someone claims to "need" something when, in reality, they are merely wanting it. For instance, I adore purchasing equipment. I can find a purpose for almost every tool here on Earth. However, I can assure you that I do not require a tool, no matter how much I would like one.

To get to work, I have to buy petrol. To ensure our family's continued health and nourishment, my spouse and I must shop for groceries. I am responsible for our insurance, utilities, and rent. Anything more than that is merely a desire.

To cut living expenses, you must understand the distinction between necessities and wants.

Investing: What Is It?

Making your money work for you is possible with investing. It's like planting a seed today to grow a bigger tree tomorrow. Simply put, it is investing your money in resources or ventures with the hope of making a profit in the future.

When you contribute, you purchase with the hope that it will be appreciated. This "something" could be anything from real estate to stocks and bonds to starting a business. Making more money than you initially invested is the goal.

Below is a summary of the key concepts in investing:

1. Assets are the things that you invest money in. Resources can be theoretical, like stocks or bonds, or substantial, like a house or jewellery. Over time, resource value might fluctuate, making investment exciting.

2. Returns: The profit you receive from your investments is this. It might appear as pay (such as interest from bonds or stock earnings) or capital gains (the increase in the resource's value). The reward for taking up the difficulty of investing is returns.

3. Risk: Investing is unquestionably an unreliable way to make money. You risk losing

all your money or perhaps just a portion of it. Diverse investment types correspond with varying levels of risk. Generally speaking, there is a strong correlation between risk and possible return; investments with higher risk have the potential to provide bigger returns, but there is also a greater chance of losing money.

4. Diversification: Many investors distribute their funds over various assets to manage risk. We refer to this as an improvement. It protects your entire portfolio since if one investment underperforms, the others may make up for it.

5. Time Skyline: Your time skyline should align with your investing goals. If you only need the money for a short period(for a rainy day account, for example), you could choose safer and more flexible assets. If you're investing for retirement, you can handle greater hurdles because you have longer recollections of bold and less promising market times.

6. Research: Completing your studies is essential before investing. Understand the resource you are putting money into, the dangers involved, and the real execution of it. Many people consult financial counsellors or use Internet resources to make educated decisions.

7. Patience: Investing is a time-consuming endeavour. Resources can be expensive daily, but it's important to stick to your long-term goals and not let short-term market changes deter you.

8. Compound Interest: This may be the most important investing concept. Over time, your money increases significantly when you receive investment returns and reinvested profits.

Do you not feel persuaded yet? Like Skinner's description of habits, Charles DuHigg's "The Power of Habit" is well-known. According to him, behaviours (operant conditioning) consist of three components:

1. Ah,

2. Typical

3. Reward

The signal initiates a habit. Maybe there's the fragrance of barbecued steak. If you've been raised to detest meat or are a vegetarian, you will not feel comfortable. But if you like steak, you'll probably be craving more.

Behaviour is routine. You may strive to avoid steak odours because you detest them. If you love the smell of grilled steak, you may head to the grocery store and get a steak to grill or dine at one of the restaurants there. The thing that strengthens a habit or behaviour is reward.

You'll be able to observe how this idea affects your habits and behaviour. Think about the impact of your emotions on your actions (both before and after the trigger). When you examine your routines, cues, and incentives, you'll be shocked at how many of your behaviours are the product of your emotions.

If you are upset, you shouldn't go shopping. We refer to this as the cue. Anxiety or discomfort is the emotion that sets off the behaviour or pattern. In this case, buying provides momentary relief as the reward. At one point, this helped to ease those emotions. Your mind is now trained to think that it will succeed every time.

You can alter your behaviour if you do something different and receive the same reward. This transition may be challenging or even sluggish. This calls for some thought and short-term giving up. Attempting something new can be intimidating at times. Consider the following questions for yourself:

Which cues in your life result in bad habits or erroneous beliefs?

What is the incentive for engaging in bad behaviour?

Can a positive habit that yields the same reward be established?

Make an effort to define a budget. Make a spending plan as opposed to a budget. Change the way you think about sustaining it. Boring chores like monitoring, checking, and reconciling don't need to cross your mind. Instead, consider phrases like tracking your progress, calculating your earnings, or determining your distance from your objective.

Making a budget and tracking your progress requires work. However, you will get the benefits if you think it is worth it. You won't attempt it and will steer clear if you think it's not worth it. It's critical to reconsider your present strategy and adopt new perspectives.

Maybe you believe making a budget is too difficult or unattainable. The techniques in this book can assist you in breaking bad behaviours. This could even lead to the formation of a new habit.

ACTION ITEM

Before beginning any of these, you should consider your options.

Spending plans and budget. Think back. Your patterns can be ascertained by analysing your operant conditioning. These patterns determine your reaction to triggers. You need to recognise these patterns if you want to alter your behaviour.

Cues set off the behaviour.

Even though you could have beliefs and ideas about your behaviour, they don't reflect who you are. But your aspirations will be revealed by the things you buy. You can identify one of your poor spending patterns with the help of this activity. Next, determine which incentive is responsible for this behaviour. The next action is to examine the prize. You can use these inquiries to gauge whether it's worth your time:

1. What was the prize? 2. For the prize, what did you have to give up?

3. How did you feel at the time? How long will it last? It may sound odd, but you should begin with the outcome or the reward. Proceed back towards the cue after that. Keeping the reward, the behaviour that earned it, and the trigger distinct is necessary. Consider whether you could get the same result by acting differently. Could the cue trigger a different behaviour and a reward akin to the one you received?

Later in this book, you'll discover a few strategies for altering the behaviour. This experimentation aims to develop a good habit (habit) that yields rewards equivalent to those of the habit you were employing. Make an effort to pinpoint your most potent triggers and significant rewards.

101st Spending Plan

One of the most important steps in altering financial habits is reprogramming your thought process. One method to accomplish this is to rearrange the framework. After reading this chapter, you'll be able to reconsider the definitions you used to detest.

When "financial experts" refer to disposable income, it irritates me. They use this disparaging term to refer to the amount of money you have left over after covering all your expenses. I find nothing wrong with this description. They force you to utilise this term, which unwittingly sets you up for failure. How?

Disposable income can only be used for one thing. It can be thrown away like any other worthless object. I propose substituting discretionary income for disposable income. Discretionary income can be used for anything—saving, investing, buying, donating, or doing nothing. There's only one place where disposable income goes. While discretionary money is only usable when available, disposable income can be allocated in various ways.

Create A Budget

You can stay organized if you stick to your budget. Annual costs like auto insurance, which displays your financial flow, won't surprise you. Unexpected expenses will also not surprise you because they are budgeted for in your spending plan.

A budget consists of two parts: revenue and expenses.

Cash received as pay, commission, dividends, interest, child support, pension, or disability benefits is referred to as income. The items you must pay for are referred to as expenses; they are not the money you generate.

Auto payments, phone bills, and homeowner's insurance premiums.

A few changeable expenses are clothing, entertainment, food, and gas.

Avoid estimating your spending, taking shortcuts, and criticizing your budget when it doesn't work because you used incorrect information or neglected to include infrequent costs (insurance, hockey fees, property taxes). It's true in terms of budgeting. Additionally, leave it alone if you're not ready to put in the time and effort required to build a realistic budget and modify it when your situation changes! Reviewing your past purchases is the best method for figuring out your expenses.

Compile your spending information for the previous six months, broken down by category (e.g., utilities, food, clothing, child care, gifts).

Divide the total by six after adding the totals for each category. That is your monthly average. Add them all together. The amount of money you have been using is that. The steps are as follows: Purchase a budget spreadsheet; mortgage payments are essential, but so are other expenses like cable and a phone. It may be necessary to part with those nice-to-haves.

1. A savings account is necessary. Clear your debt and maintain a contingency account. For now, don't bother saving anything.

2. A Reduction in Variable Expenses: As mentioned before, certain things are pleasant. You need to eat and have access to transportation to get to work. Decide if you can afford to take a taxi or buy organic groceries.

3. Pay attention to the revenue.

If there are still gaps in the budget, you must make some cuts. Lower the amounts for your variable expenses first. Some items you may need to part with include video games, alcohol, cigarettes, mani-pedis, haircuts, coffee, lunch meals, and mani-pedis if you are in debt.

The entertainment budget will cover everything, including your sports involvement. You're able to buy ground beef. Everyone should eat properly, but to do so, you have to be very careful, buy only items that are in season, use coupons, and make every bite count. Additionally, no one is allowed to eat out!

4. Examine your fixed expenses next. Cut back on your electricity, cable, and phone expenses. Sync up your auto and home insurance. Raise the amount of your deductible.

Cut back on the price of your insurance. If you have children that just won't stop growing, there are times when an article of clothing crosses the line from good to acceptable when your only pair of winter boots breaks.

After adding a must-have number to cover the necessities, you enhance it to a nice-to-have number for all the extras you want. If you ever need to make cuts, it's nice to have.

5. Be Realistic, not Idealistic. If you reduce spending in one area to balance the budget, remember you will still need to make purchases. If you don't include things like clothing, maintenance of the house, leisure, family gifts, and auto repairs, you're not being

practical. 6. Prepare to immediately alter your route. Things happen, and sometimes you have to spend money. If the amount in your "vehicle repair" fund isn't sufficient to pay for the tires, you might have to buy new ones.

You soon "borrow" funds from your budget for house upkeep. It is a fact that your income cannot exceed your expenses. You need to either increase your income or cut costs if you cannot get the budget to balance. Debt repayment is required.

Set aside money for emergencies as well as long-term needs.

If you think you can always make decisions on the fly, good luck. We appreciate your decision to take charge of your financial destiny.

By creating a balanced budget, you've taken a big step towards managing your finances better.

I consider my budget a sacred book that helps me stay honest. I can assess whether my current expenditure reflects a change in circumstances or if, when I reviewed my past spending, I was not paying enough attention.

My finances do not dictate who I am. If, for one month, I overindulge in entertainment, I look for areas where I may make cuts. I make the decision.

Section 4:

Do not use your debit or credit card.

◆◆◆

Synopsis: Most college students view obtaining their first credit card as a milestone. This is how your credit is first created. You can also increase your financial independence by doing this. However, many students are unaware that, similar to having a stellar GPA, having a solid credit history is quite important for their prospects. If they want to avoid paying a large sum of money after or before graduation, students still need to learn how to keep their credit or debit cards hidden.

Obtaining a credit card and applying for every credit card offer—available to all students—are completely different things. You must think about student loans if you're a student. So, resist the temptation to accept every free T-shirt offer.

How Not to Use Your Credit or Debit Card.

This is because using your credit card to its full potential will result in more expenses. Avoiding overspending on something you cannot afford is fundamental to money management. It is easier to accumulate large debt that you will find difficult to pay off if you have certain credit cards.

Using your money to buy your necessities is one of these tactics. Use the cash you still have in your pocket or wallet instead of your credit card. You'll be able to avoid using your credit card by doing this. However, this does not mean that credit card use is bad. You can always make use of them but don't mistreat them. Abusing credit or debit cards may be extremely disastrous, particularly for those who use them frequently for purchases.

Another strategy to avoid credit cards is to stay away from places where you could be tempted to buy study-related necessities. Avoid using debit or credit cards all the time to pay for your schooling. Consider it your option if you can pay for it with cash or a loan. Even using a credit card could benefit you by building your credit history and not meeting your payments on time credit history.

Understanding or being aware of credit cards is also essential prior to applying for one. This might help you think through what actions to take or not take to resolve any issues.

Section Three

THE SCIENCE OF PARTYING

Among the skills that have the power to completely transform a person is becoming the best at assignments. The problem with many individuals, especially women, is that they almost always assume they're the only ones who can follow through on an assignment and do it as effectively as possible. But keep in mind that "right" is often an emotive term. Maybe someone else can handle it perfectly.

By using other people's time, we should be able to identify a few things that will help you succeed in your designation and enhance your life.

Transfer the Correct Kind of Tasks

Make heads or tails of the comparatively large number of errands you run first once you have them all sorted and organized.

Sometimes, you can use innovation to computerize them, but other times, you'll need to find someone else to handle the task.

Assign the Correct Person to the Tasks

You'll need to find the correct person for that task and assign the appropriate errands. If you know someone who is already excellent at the task you should be finishing, they are the most appropriate candidate to join since they are certain to know how to

Execute it. You just hand it over to them and let them take care of the rest. If you come into someone who hasn't done it before, you'll have to prepare them. That makes sense if your budget is smaller, but hiring an expert will make things easier.

Go ahead.

Move as soon as you hand over the errand to someone else. Don't worry about it excessively. Give them a few suppositions for the task, without a doubt. If you hire someone to clean your house, for example, be sure to let them know what matters to you so they can consider the cleaning job done properly. Then, let them finish.

Since most specialized companies already have a specific method for completing that task, given their level of expertise, it's usually best to let them proceed after you've agreed upon expectations.

Make Use of Your Newfound Free Time

It's not enough to assign an errand to someone else; that is obvious. If all else is equal, use the extra time you have to do a worthwhile task. You will feel much more valuable and appreciate setting aside more time if you use that time to accomplish something important to you, like spending time with your partner, kids, friends, or profitable errands. Is there a solid reason you wouldn't appoint someone else to do something they could do more quickly, for less money, and with an equivalent level of quality (or nearly as good) as you? It is pointless to continue if, on the odd chance, you feel overwhelmed because you are doing too much. Invest time and energy in being ready and delegating to others, as you'll be improving your own life and possibly theirs.

AUTOMATION AND MECHANISATION THAT WILL SAVE YOU TIME

Computerizing the things you might be able to do is one way to become more valuable. You can mechanize many things these days, both in business and your personal life.

We ought to consider a few ideas that could greatly impact your day and make it far more focused on employing creativity and constructive routines.

Configure Your Devices Correctly

If your PC is programmed appropriately, it can maintain its own pace. Configure your computer to update automatically, thereby scanning for malware and maintaining system cleanliness. There are options for you to learn about, regardless of whether you own a Mac or a PC.

Use the Bill Payment System at Your Bank to Pay Your Bills

Nowadays, you may set up automatic payment options directly through the majority of Mastercards and charges, but using your bank's system to set them up is a better approach

and a more organized way to go about it because, if you truly want to make a change, it's everywhere. The installment process can be automated. Today's banks provide this assistance at no cost as well.

Plan Meals Digitally with a Dinner Kit

If planning and buying for a feast takes a lot of effort, you can automate a good portion of this by choosing a feast unit delivery service. After that, they'll notify you via email before each shipment of the other items you need to buy. At that point, you can also create a request for your local supermarket and even automate some of that process using Amazon's Subscribe and Save options.

Eliminate Paper

If you find yourself with a lot of desk work regularly, try to learn how to go paperless. When searching, paperless documents are easier to locate than other kinds of records. If you learn how to use your PC, you can also get it to do some of this automatically.

You may also learn how to use Zapier.com to automate many recording capabilities, both at home and at work. It's categorized as "Automator on the Mac," while on Windows, it's called "Activities on Windows."

Day 8

B

Before we go any further, let's dispel the myth that a secret formula determines how much money you should have saved by age X (or any other age, for that matter). Naturally, having a $1,000,000 bank account when you're fifty sounds wonderful, but in many situations, this is incredibly impossible. Your savings rate, or the percentage of money you save compared to your income, is far more significant and practical than the total amount you save.

Although it may be tempting to use the excuse "I'm not making enough money" to put off saving money, the true impact of savings lies in the percentage of money saved rather than the amount saved. Consider this if you are saving very little and find it discouraging to consider how little you can save each month: if you set aside 1/10 of your monthly income, you will have 36.5 days free from paying income taxes after a year. You can live on that amount of savings for more than a month. Even if you only save 20% of your income, you will still have enough savings to last 18 days without working; if you reach a savings target of 1% of your income, you will have enough savings to last 73 days annually.

You see, that is one benefit of examining your savings rate instead of a fixed amount. Since everyone has different spending habits, having $1,000,000 in the bank might not be the best goal to concentrate on if your expenses and income levels are significantly lower anyway.

Here's another method to demonstrate the potency of a savings rate (SR):

You can save $150 a month and live off $1,350 in expenses if your monthly income is $1,500 net and you achieve a savings rate of 10%.

Conversely, if you reach an SR of 20%, you can live on $1,200 and save $300 a month.

Now, imagine that after three years of doing this, your income suddenly stops coming in each month, and you lose your job. The aforementioned scenarios would play out as follows:

After three years (thirty-six months) with an SR of 10%, you would have saved $5,400. This buffer would last for four months if you had to rely solely on it because you are accustomed to living on $1,350 (assuming your expenses stay the same).

After three years, with a 20% SR, your savings would be $10,800. You could sustain yourself for nine months on $1,200 a month if you were to live on that amount.

In the event of need, a twice as large SR (20% as opposed to 10%) would last more than twice as long because an increased SR has the dual effect of increasing savings and decreasing spending.

Naturally, the above illustration is oversimplified a little bit because your savings consist of more than just the money you put into savings accounts—they also include any contributions you make to longer-term savings like your retirement account or accounts you may have for private investments. Ultimately, these also hold money that you are saving for the future and didn't spend today. In other words, even though those contributions aren't readily available in a bank account to use in the event that your income disappears, they would still be considered savings.

Keeping that in mind, concentrate on the portion of your income that you set aside for savings instead of getting too worked up about how much you make and save.

The Reasons And Methods Of Marketing

Before I begin, let me mention this straight away. The focus of internet marketing is on the customer, not on you or your goods. Instead, it is on the customer and the value you are providing. Social networking is still the most widely used platform for friends to connect with friends, and it's a terrific method for customers to stay in touch with your company. Almost everyone on the internet is familiar with the seven social networking sites, and they have essentially taken over as people's go-to places.

The most popular websites for drawing visitors to your website are YouTube, Twitter, Instagram, Facebook, TikTok, Reddit, and Google (blogs). It's crucial to have a presence on each of these platforms, but keep in mind that new websites are being added daily and becoming increasingly popular. It's critical to keep in mind why individuals utilize social networking sites as a means of communication with the outside world.

This is something you should consider when you develop your Internet marketing plan. You are aware of the difficulties if you have ever had a friend or family member who participated in network marketing. Have you ever had to break off all communication with any "friends" because they incessantly discussed their "opportunity"? Try to avoid that and keep your personal and commercial social media accounts apart. Their failure to end the business spiel could ultimately cause them to lose the connection. You do not want it to occur due to your social networking strategy.

Visitors to your website are indeed aware that you are a product vendor. Still, you also need to strike a balance between making money from your social networking sites and providing valuable resources. DO YOUR RESEARCH because this balance may vary based on the kind of business you own. Asking yourself, "Would I enjoy visiting my site?" is the most important question. Answering that question is difficult. However, you must ask and respond to the question: will you purchase from this website? If not, get to work improving it. It will get better every day.

Remembering the fundamentals is critical— never overdoing anything, but also realizing that other people are involved. Make your commercial something that people will enjoy and won't feel compelled to buy every time they see it since people like to surf the internet and buy stuff, but they don't like to be sold to. Remember these guidelines when you create your social media plan.

In conclusion, be present everywhere, and don't be afraid to take risks. That piques viewers' interest and encourages them to purchase your goods out of choice rather than coercion.

Chapter 6: Act

Email marketing is done correctly.

Email marketing, always looking at things from a financial standpoint, is, in my opinion, a huge help to your bottom line. Emails are faster and more efficient than snail mail, but in the recent past, businesses had to pay for printing, paper, and postage to stay in touch with their customers. Don't be fooled; offline mail order is still relevant today, and offline marketing has a place when creating an internet business's long-term plan.

Specifically, though, when done well, email marketing can be incredibly effective. People ignore most of their emails because they receive far too many spam messages. An email marketing effort is doomed if emails end up in the spam folder because once you're in there, people stop trusting you. Sending spam emails could also be the final blow to your bank account. There's no way your online business can afford to ignore compliance with new rules, especially when U.S. government laws are going to make it more illegal for Internet marketers to send unsolicited emails.

The greatest way to ensure that everyone getting your emails has chosen to do so voluntarily is to, at the very least, use your auto-responder tool. Therefore, I advise against sending unsolicited emails to anyone. The last thing you want is to irritate a possible client with unsolicited emails. Simply deliver them to people who are ready to accept them.

Regarding email marketing, remember that the main goal is to establish offers, greetings, and other emails that don't seem to be trying to get them to buy your stuff. Who doesn't give a damn about your business is not your aim. Maintaining contact with perhaps a few hundred of your clientele is your aim, as is providing prospective clients with the most recent information about your offerings.

I've done a lot of study and have developed the following guidelines for email marketing:

Keep in mind that an impression makes an impression. Write your first email with great care. Enroll in your email service and check your messages as soon as they arrive. What is the appearance? Would you click on it as an uninterested customer? Will you respond to that email? Ask yourself these questions. Your first email will arrive shortly after the customer subscribes to your list, increasing the likelihood that they will open and read it. But if you don't catch their eye with this initial email and deliver them anything of value, they won't likely open anymore from you. I think I would give them a discount offer or anything useful to entice them to buy your stuff.

The content's quality ought to come first. Individuals read emails to obtain knowledge that will benefit them in their daily lives or enterprises. They don't read emails trying to pitch you on a product that will make your life easier. Make sure your material is of a high caliber so that recipients of your emails genuinely look forward to receiving them each week. Subheadings, bulleted lists, and brief paragraphs can divide the text and improve its readability and presentation.

Take care not to set unrealistic expectations for the reader. Since sending them many emails is the idea, don't create unrealistic expectations for yourself, but don't keep it too low either. Strike a balance. A series of mediocre emails after one outstanding one is preferable to underpromising and overdelivering.

Every email should have value added to it, even if that means offering something for free. You don't have to pay anything to receive the free item. It might be a tip from your experience, such as a fantastic website, a complimentary report, or a discount code for future purchases. Remember that everything related to you and your company, even free, ought to be of the greatest caliber because it will help the client feel valued and special.

In the email body, invite recipients to engage with you. People prefer not to read endlessly without engaging with the content, so link to your social media accounts or provide them a clickable link to additional content.

Give the email's title some thought. Observe how the email appears on the different Internet-browsing technologies that individuals use, such as smartphones and other portable devices. You need to capture their interest within the first few words of your title. Explain in the email's subject line why they must open and read your message.

Optimising Work and Productivity: Putting your physical space in order

Keeping your physical space organized is similar to leading a peaceful, effective symphony. It's the ability to arrange your environment to meet your needs, interests, and goals. Start by eliminating anything unnecessary and retaining only the things that make you happy. Organize your stuff so it's easy to find what you need and function properly. Use storage solutions like shelves, drawers, and bins to sort and arrange items based on their importance and use. Make your space reflect what you do regularly by keeping less often used items properly stored and frequently used goods within easy reach. In addition to enhancing productivity and mental clarity, a neatly arranged physical area also acts as a haven of harmony and order.

minimizing interruptions and distractions

The key to establishing a concentrated and productive environment is to minimize interruptions and distractions so that you can concentrate on the tasks that truly count. Determine your primary sources of distraction, be they noise, electronic devices, or unexpected guests. To lessen these distractions, turn off your phone, set aside specific times to receive emails, or invest in noise-canceling headphones.

If at all possible, creating a dedicated workspace can greatly reduce disruptions. Set clear limits for uninterrupted time by communicating your work and attention times to family, roommates, or coworkers. Additionally, teach others to respect your work schedule by learning how to politely deny requests that are not urgent within your allotted concentration hours.

Additionally, adopt time management strategies to organize your day and set aside dedicated time for specific projects, such as the Pomodoro Technique and Time Blocking. Setting out specified time slots for working on particular projects may lessen the possibility of job switching and keep your workflow consistent. Turn off all alerts and focus on the task during these concentrated periods. Additionally, schedule "catch-up" or "open-door" meetings to address little problems or unforeseen requests, grouping disruptions into predetermined times.

Including mindfulness exercises can help with distraction management as well. You can minimize the impact of distractions by swiftly identifying when your attention wanders and bringing it back to it. Reducing interruptions and distractions ultimately comes down to intentionally creating your workspace and routines to safeguard your concentration, allowing you to complete things quickly and feel in control of your time and output.

Advice Nos. 6 through 10

6. Clarify What You Mean by Wealth

A common misconception is that having a solid basis of income equates to wealth. In actuality, it is possible for someone to earn a lot of money but have a net worth of nothing due to heavy debt. This is not affluent. Your ability to pay cash for necessities and the amount of debt you own are the key indicators of wealth.

7-Make Good Use of Your Time

Or, to put it another way, individuals who get up early will be financially independent. You must get up earlier and work efficiently, particularly if time is of the essence. Use that time to study financial independence strategies or take concrete steps towards achieving it.

8- Give emergency fund savings a priority.

Debt repayment is wonderful, but you should establish an emergency fund first. This might be a fixed number, like $1,000, or a range, like the cost of living for one to three months. This is a safety net if you must pay off debt due to unforeseen circumstances.

9- Monitor Your Money

You have to be very careful about tracking every dollar you spend if you are serious about achieving financial freedom. There is no other method to determine whether you have leaks or places that need tightening. Maintain a ledger where you can track all of your earnings and expenses. Additionally, save your receipts for any purchases you make at shops, services, etc.

10-Stop Expenditure

List the necessities you must pay for and the frivolous items you buy monthly, including any rendered services. You might be able to cut back on some expenses and use the money to pay off debt or establish an emergency fund. If you want to succeed, one of the first things you should do is this.

They Make Too Many Payment Method Attempts

Personal finance gets more difficult the more complicated your financial situation is. If you'll pardon me for a moment, I'd like you to imagine a society where credit cards and the ability to borrow money are nonexistent.

For anything they wished to buy, everyone would have to pay cash. Can you picture how simple your money might become as a result?

Things get more complicated with more credit cards and loans on file. You find yourself spending money on six different credit cards with different balances before you realize it.

Then, you'll need to open multiple accounts to pay for all those goods. It's also quite challenging to determine exactly how much money you have and how much you owe because every account has a different interest rate and broadcasts transactions at different times. It's a disorganized approach to managing your money, usually resulting in poor spending choices and mistakes.

Conversely, if you only make purchases using a debit card, you can access a single account and see exactly how much money you have. This makes keeping track of your spending easier and budgeting more enjoyable overall.

They have debt from credit cards.

It's no secret, in my opinion, that credit card debt is bad news. As mentioned, it complicates your spending patterns and has the added stomach-punching of high interest rates.

You risk being in credit card debt indefinitely if you don't make a concerted effort to pay them off due to the exorbitant interest rates.

The biggest enemy of financial success is credit card debt, which is also a major contributing factor to the high number of bankruptcies.

They Take Out Loans To Buy Deteriorating Assets.

Apart from having credit card debt, the majority of people live in poverty because they take out loans to cover large purchases they cannot afford.

Furthermore, most loans are taken out to purchase depreciating items like

vehicles, recreational vehicles, boats, and almost anything else powered by a motor. Although I'm not a finance expert, I think the key to wealth is investing in things that increase in value rather than paying more for items that depreciate.

They Use Cash Flow to Guide Their Financial Decisions

Relying solely on the monthly payment amount to determine whether or not you can afford something is one of the most common financial mistakes people make.

For example, "I can afford the monthly payment; therefore, I can afford it" if you wish to purchase a new car.

In the interim, a rich viewpoint may be,

"I can't afford this automobile, since I can't pay for it altogether."

It's easy to become bankrupt if you base your purchases on the amount of the monthly payments—interest included or not.

Why? Because monthly payments will eventually exhaust your income, and worse, you will be obligated to make those payments for a period of time extending into months or even years.

Buying things based only on cash flow and monthly payments is akin to progressively sending oneself to bankruptcy.

They Don't Stock Up On Emergency Supplies

A 2018 Federal Reserve Board study found that almost one-third of American families would have to borrow or sell something to pay for an emergency.

I don't know about you, but it seems like a significant problem. In particular, an emergency doesn't seem ordinary to me. In my opinion, that is a typical event in life.

You are setting yourself up for financial disaster if you don't prepare for these emergencies. Apart from health crises, what happens if your car breaks down? What happens if you get fired? The worst part is that you will encounter more emergencies the less prepared you are.

But it won't cost you anything more than a little aggravation if you are organized, plan, and set aside some cash for that emergency.

Exercise 5: Completing the Whole

Now that you've studied, ranked, and examined everything, it's time to bring everything together.

At this point, you start actively managing your finances. Some people may have found the preceding exercises discouraging when they realized they were constantly overspending or that their income was insufficient to pay their expenditures. "How am I supposed to find extra money if there isn't any extra?" one may wonder. The following sections go into great detail about "finding" more money, but the most important thing to remember is to create and implement a money management plan right now.

The only time you are promised is right now, so avoid saying things like, "I'll do it when I make more money." You have to start where you are to see a brighter financial future. To make it true tomorrow, own it today in whichever manner you can.

STEP 1A:

Control your reckless spending and have fun at the same time. Spending doesn't have to be eliminated. Start by giving yourself a challenge to reduce your 10% thoughtless expenditure. After you routinely accomplish that goal, push yourself to a greater proportion. In the upcoming parts, we'll talk about several ways to save costs without sacrificing quality of life.

STEP 1B:

Leave your credit cards at home if you struggle with impulsive credit card spending. You can determine whether that "gotta have" item is necessary by taking the extra time to go back and grab the credit card. Recall that you cannot settle the debt if you keep adding to it.

Step 2:

Start allocating a certain sum of money as an emergency fund. A reserve of 10% of your income is ideal. If that's too ambitious, figure out how much you can save from every paycheck, even if it's just $5 or $10 at a time. You will keep adding to this emergency fund until the balance reaches $10,000, or six months' worth of your income, whichever is higher. Should you require access to it, you will pledge to reimburse it. This is meant to be a real emergency fund, utilized in the event of a disaster to prevent taking on more debt. A family wedding or even a vacation cannot compare to a disaster. A crisis is an expensive auto repair, a medical emergency, or something similar. This fund is intended to help you escape financial difficulties that arise from life's obstacles so that you won't have to suffer any longer.

Step 3:

Ten percent of your salary should go towards debt repayment. The distinction between debts and expenses must be made in this case. Expenses are the things associated with living essentials, such as food, transportation, utilities, etc. Debts are things you voluntarily took on and are not essential to existence. Take credit cards, for instance. If you regularly pay for everyday expenses with a credit card, there might be some questions about that description, but the debt is still there regardless of why it occurred.

If you are unable to begin allocating 10% of your income to debt repayment, set a goal that you will progressively raise until the debt is settled or 10% of your income is available. It is not how much you start with that matters, but rather that you start.

Start by making payments on the credit card or other debt you listed first in Exercise 3, Step 1. For all other credit cards and debts, make the minimal payment. Here, apply any difference from paying the minimum on the other cards to the highest priority item and add the money you set aside in the previous step to pay off your debt. This should be done repeatedly until the initial card is paid off.

As soon as it's paid, take the amount you paid on the first card and apply it to the next, being sure to add it to the minimum payment. For instance, you might have set aside $100 a month to pay off your top debt, which requires a minimum payment of $100. The minimum payment required for the second card on your list was $200. Following the payment for the first item, you will now pay for the second item, which is $400. You will take that $400 and apply it to the minimum payment when the third one is due, and so on.

If you have any extra cash for your bills

Once your invoices are paid, upload them to see your savings. Create an emergency fund if you have unforeseen expenses (such as a furnace breaking in January). The more you store, the faster you'll attain your financial objectives.

Keeping Your Budget in Balance

Your finances might not stabilize when you first try budgeting if you're not experienced with it. You should look for areas where you could save costs and make changes along the route.

A method for setting up and managing a financing

Many American households have a terrible perception of budgeting, believing it to be a way to take all the fun out of spending money. No greater purchasing. No more overindulging at restaurants. Weekend golfing is out.

That isn't the reason for a budget's motive.

A budget displays the amount of money coming in and the expenditure of that money. It helps you get the most out of your money, making it one of the most important tools in creating a prosperous financial future.

All customers, no matter their financial situation or generation, can gain from making and managing a budget. Finance gives people a sense of control over their financial resources. Think of finance as the economic foundation. Everybody has a unique foundation, just as every financial position is unique.

Selecting a Tool for Budgeting

There are four main methods to establish, track, and oversee finances. Although every gadget employs a different approach, they focus on agency and element awareness.

The most traditional and least opulent approach to budgeting is using a notebook and pen. If they are in balance, you can proceed.

The Spreadsheet: Microsoft Excel is the most often used spreadsheet application for budgeting. Instead of asking users to construct their own Excel budgeting worksheets, many websites offer free samples of the forms. A spreadsheet handles the calculations and makes it easy to prepare large amounts of data.

Free Internet software: There are several free web-based programs that can help with budgeting. You may establish and categorize your prices with these packages, like Manilla and Mint.Com, and track your spending to see exactly where your money is going as soon as the transaction is made.

Economic software programs: These apps also exist, although using them requires some computer skills. The primary product is Quicken.

The well-known economist Dave Ramsey suggests a zero-based budgeting method in which you set aside all your funds in advance at the beginning of each month using envelopes.

You might also check with your nearby bank or credit union for tips and advice. To help you get started, your savings group may also provide budgeting worksheets. You can select the U.S. Many budgeting worksheets and materials are available from the Financial Literacy and Education Fee (FLEC), which may assist you at any stage.

Making a Spending Plan

Techniques and strategies for budgeting are diverse. For instance, what works for a retiree and what works for a first-year university student may differ. Nonetheless, expanding a financial company only requires five easy procedures. They're all essential because they reinforce one another and aid in the sensible organization of your finances.

Step 1: Make objectives

You must decide which objectives address necessities and which ones deal with extravagance. You can then order your financial priorities as a result.

One of the immediate financial needs is to safeguard current expenses. A few of these are required, such as your rent or mortgage payment, auto loans, utility bills, child care, food, phone, and household goods. Discretionary gadgets, or secondary desires, include non-essential clothing, subscription services, eating out, and vacations. Long-term financial goals may involve investments, retirement funds, and charitable giving. If you have debt, paying it off could be required and optional. Financial solvency depends on making the appropriate payments, but it may make more sense in the long run to pay off debt early when it is no longer necessary.

Step 2: Determine your income and expenses

Before attempting this, you should assess your income and fees because maximum bills have a month-to-month schedule.

Revenue sources, such as your pay (after taxes), regular bonuses, and expenses related to child support or spousal maintenance. You might use an estimate if you're unsure about the precise amount. After obtaining your figures, sum them up. The whole is what you make each month.

The next component of the calculation is your charges, divided into three categories: variable-committed costs, constant-committed charges, and discretionary-committed charges.

Fixed devoted prices: these include your mortgage or rent and have a set monthly sum.

Variable dedicated fee: This would include groceries and petrol and varies from month to month, mostly depending on necessity.

Discretionary costs include undertaking and leisure and are, as previously said, non-compulsory. A subscription to a gym may also be considered in this group. Discretionary expenses can add extra satisfaction to lives, but they should go first if you can't afford the necessities.

You will begin to spend a great deal of interest if you don't repay your monthly credit card payments. This might cause chaos for any budget. Remember to consult with a nonprofit credit counselor if your overdue credit card payments account for more than 10% of your monthly income. An informal credit counseling consultation over the phone or online will review your finances and suggest possible cost reductions or eliminations. You might be able to reduce your monthly debt payments if you are eligible for a debt management program.

Was Necessary

My grandparents, in my opinion, invented a wholly American civilization. Custom. Their will to take possession of the land, rely on themselves, and build a wealthy existence reflects the bravery and drive at the core of the American ideal. The initial Europeans were motivated by these aspirations. Immigrants leave their familiar environment of comfort and confidence behind to enter a foreign and possibly dangerous new world. My ancestors came to these beaches for various reasons and in extremely different situations. He was surrounded by visions of self-determination and deep versatility for a while, which inspired my forebears to work hard and pursue their aspirations.

-At one point, they were in the position to do so.

My curiosity has been stifled by my ancestors' experiences, such as the internal discrepancies I can see within comparatively short presentation times because of where my grandmother and grandfather arrived. How come we, as a collective culture, have traveled such a big distance so quickly? Are there any internal psychology lessons to be learned from the wheel of fortune that can be applied to travel?

Many Europeans who fought their way over the Atlantic were searching for a way to start a new life without being subject to the internal authority of their native kingdom. The ability to hunt, cultivate their land, provide for their families, and practice their preferred religion marked a turning point in one's quality of life. The freedom they discovered illustrates a certain kind of fortune that is priceless and eternal throughout all cultures.

But we do know that these immigrants and their descendants' lives were hard, at times even lethal, for the first 150 years or more. Until then, numerous facilities were available to people in Europe, especially those in the lower classes of society. Satisfying the most basic needs was a daily occurrence in this strange new land. Activate. Many people were abruptly reduced to evaluating their status in life based only on the most basic criteria—access to food, shelter, and physical safety. line between life and death, such as this one, occasionally depends on internal climate changes and potential disruptions to food supplies. Because of this, the major American economic development periods from 1607 to 1790— which can best be characterized as "was from base need"—may be best described as inside. The majority believed that dominion over the land and its produce was a sign of both survival and success.

Land Of Opportunity = Earthly Opportunity

IN THE rural economy of Young Peace development, Like in many parts of the Old World, owning land provided the greatest chance for success. Most people relied on agriculture for their daily needs and future financial prospects. Some engaged in commerce with Native Americans or exported commodities to Europe. However, success for the average person meant owning a house like this, a few heads of cattle, and a garden large enough to produce enough food for their family. It was also necessary to have a horse and cart to transport you and your supplies to and from the city. Having multiple horses, such as this extra crop for sale, was excess.

America possesses large ones, like this one Earth from potential, for a good cause. Farewell to most of the new Americans who established themselves using customs and the richest resources he possessed from vast amounts of Earth. For wealthy families, the enormous tracts of undeveloped property in the Americas offered practically endless possibilities. The nobles of the New World, the owners of the largest extensions, could generate an excess of food and offer staff services. This excess production made the earliest financial fortune accumulation within the Young World possible.

The Europeans who made up this New World nobility were granted rights to large land areas in the colonies. The governments of Spain, the Netherlands, and England purchased or seized hundreds of thousands of hectares of Native American land, promising them a high position or influence among European households. Additionally, cards were promised to companies like the Massachusetts Bay Company, whose operations could help the motherland. The wealth of the receivers of these grants increased rapidly, and they had complete control over the income generated from within Earth (even though they were also heavily taxed cities). This site granted the owners' relatives and their descendants the right to possess, sell, inherit, or bequeath their land and the ability to buy more Earth from other people in some English-founded colonies in the east.

The climate in the southern colonies proved ideal for the growth of large plantations and farms. As the American colonies' populations increased, agriculture gained ground in the South, while this industry expanded most readily in the North.

Southern planters increased production by using slave labor, believing this would benefit the United States. The pre-war South saw the emergence of an aristocratic way of life. American wealth was booming, according to those landowners from that era.

A second wave of well-connected immigrants arrived as cities and settlements grew in the American colonies. After relocating to the northeast, some well-off immigrants started businesses that eventually garnered them enormous fortunes, such as banks for investments and exchange services. These new

Americans established partnerships and economic alliances that maintained their money and assets within their immediate families, or at the very least close to a circle of acquaintances, to preserve their power and influence. These economic behemoths occasionally provided background information on the American Revolution and the ensuing Civil War. As an illustration of its enormous financial resources and extraordinary luck, consider the Young World's expansion throughout the first two centuries.

Although there were significant economic gaps in early America between wealthy landowners and people who farmed the land, the yearning for self-determination had already begun to impact many of the first immigrants to this hemisphere. Executing this desire by many new Americans laid the foundation for a philosophy that is Stillunderlaid inside the National team conscience: life and freedom, like this inside the chase of happiness. That desire was to boost America's economic future and ignite a Wonderful world political blow from inside the American Revolution.

Chapter 2: How Lucrative Is Trading in Options?

Advantages of Options Trading

Coziness

A calm work environment enhances the quality of the output, or rather, the consequences are quite beneficial. A calm environment fosters concentration, allowing informal investors to tightly control actual day-to-day trading activities and gain more consistent knowledge. The significant benefits that would be realized ultimately show that this will fulfill their grand ambitions.

Hazard Assessment

Being exposed to regular day-to-day exchanges will enhance your courage as a person. Day trading consists of so many risks that are encountered daily. To become a successful day trader, the broker will control the bold moves and eliminate the previous mistakes.

Personal Supervisor

The greatest thing ever has been and always will be the ability to work how you want. Your plan, your actions, your strategies. This is fantastic. Imagine taking a much-needed vacation without obtaining some amazing clarification from the HR department so your justification can be adequately plausible. Additionally, starting to work for you immediately provides you with all the energy necessary to bring things to life. You have enough soul to discover and bring out the best in you. Be your boss and take care of yourself.

The drawbacks of option trading

Like anything involving accounts, there are undoubtedly disadvantages that outweigh the advantages. The same holds when trading selections. The following are some disadvantages of trading choices:

Investments for the Short Term Are Options

These are conjectures with expiration dates that range from a few months to as little as one day. This suggests that to take advantage of options, the broker needs to be prepared with a precise strategy. Generally speaking, decisions are unsuitable for a financier looking to make long-term investments.

Extra Expenses

Aside from premium payments, other costs are associated with trading options, such as commissions to finance companies, etc.

Infinite Losses

Trading decisions can expose a merchant to countless losses since, if the dealer exercises the right to the option, they must trade the relevant resource within a specific time frame.

Chapter 3: Principal Justifications for Trading Options (Why The Risk of Options Trading Is Worth It)

When you are ready to offer your money something to do for you, here are some benefits of choosing options that exchange for some of the other venture possibilities.

Reduce the Risk

You should limit your risk to how much you pay for the premium, which is a good reason to stick with your purchase decisions. When dealing with options, you don't risk losing a significant amount of money—even money you didn't contribute. This isn't the case with other venture possibilities.

More Effective Leverage for Funds

You'll notice that having options available can provide you with a lot of useful leverage. A retailer will genuinely wish to buy a choice location that closely resembles their stock position, even if doing so will result in significant cost savings.

Higher Return Percentage

To get some control over a resource, a choice dealer must pay a small portion of its value. This will enable the dealer to make more money than they otherwise might if they purchase the resource outright and then try to sell it.

Aids in Hedging Futures or Intraday Trades

Merchants typically buy or short-sell futures contracts because they believe the market will eventually move in a certain direction. The same action may be done by intraday brokers, who purchase many offers with the hope that they will rise or fall during the day. The broker may lose a lot of weight if they choose an incorrect course on the Futures or the intraday exchanges. You could lose an infinite amount of money in the process unless you are placed in a stop misfortune.

Chapter 2: Money Habits You Must Break

It might be exhilarating to start a job and enter the employment. You're prepared to pick up new abilities, use your knowledge and abilities at work, and eagerly anticipate moving up the success ladder. Having enough money to make your own financial decisions is also a bonus. Along with it comes a troubling trend in how individuals in their 20s are squandering their money.

From Bad Debts to Bad Habits

Americans owed more than $887 billion on credit cards in 2022—a $46 billion rise from the first quarter. Early financial mismanagement sets you up for future financial hardship. Unfortunately, this is a trap that many people in their 20s fall into.

They can begin with squandering money on goods that temporarily satisfy your needs but don't improve your life or financial situation in the long run. This is known as instant gratification. Consuming non-essentials to the extent that you have no money left over from your monthly income is another bad behavior.

Investing in depreciating assets or continuously participating in behaviors you cannot afford might cause serious financial difficulties. Furthermore, breaking these spending habits later on is far more difficult if they are established early on.

It takes more than just improving your money management skills. It's also not something you should address until later in life. As you get richer, your expenses will rise exponentially as well.

You may spend carelessly now, thinking you'll be able to start saving in your 30s and 40s, but by then, your spending patterns will have become second nature. You won't be able to save much money in the future due to your increased spending.

Financial gurus advise against such debt due to the following consequences: Being in debt to someone goes beyond simple debt. Clients have experienced financial, emotional, physical, and mental devastation as a result of it. I've seen individuals who were experiencing health problems as a result of the stress brought on by their debt. Some even start to deny their debt.

Negative Debt and Enhanced Liability

Having bad spending habits indicates that you are not managing your finances. It probably also signifies that you frequently have trouble waiting for your next paycheck at the end of the month and that you are unclear about where most of your money goes.

Excessive spending over your income can swiftly put you in debt. This involves making large, frequent, impulsive purchases and heavily depending on your credit card to pay for them. People who take loans and debt casually may find themselves sinking farther into debt with little effort to get out.

This is related to not meeting your financial responsibilities. Either you're delaying making the necessary payments until the last minute or employing payment options that just worsen your debt. A mismatch between your savings and debts may erode your financial freedom even more.

In my opinion, one of the most prevalent forms of bad debt among Americans is credit card debt. Most people start depending on their credit cards to make ends meet, get through the end of the month, or even just keep the lights on because of poor spending habits and financial irresponsibility.

Bad debt may be extremely crippling in several ways. It offers no advantages, complicates financial planning, and significantly depletes your income. As your liability rises, your options for financial support may become severely constrained.

Typical Poor Financial Practices

Fortunately, there is an easy and efficient way to recognize and stop spending patterns that result in bad debt:

Disregarding your credit history

Not tracking their income and expenses is one of the first bad financial habits most people in their 20s get into. More precisely, you are accruing further debt without maintaining a record of your outstanding balance. Your credit report summarizes details on your credit history and present circumstances, including the names of your creditors, credit accounts, and payment histories.

For various reasons, many people frequently forget to check their credit reports. Teenagers, in particular, may steer clear of this out of a persistent fear of what they might discover underneath. But regardless of how good or poor your credit is, failing to check it can lead to several problems.

For instance, it has been estimated that 20% of all credit reports contain some sort of inaccuracy, resulting in a lower score than anticipated. This means that you will only be eligible for higher interest rates on loans in the future.

More significantly, having an awareness of your money empowers you to take action to make improvements. Additionally, it might help you see where your financial planning is falling short and what needs to be adjusted.

Not only is your credit necessary to obtain future loans, but it can also affect other aspects of your life. For instance, prospective employers and landlords might review your report and use it to inform their conclusions about your application.

PART II COSTS

Small expenses should be avoided since they can cause a huge ship to sink.

Spending Patterns

I understand that the most difficult aspect of the PSE Report and money, in general, is the spending section; we don't get to choose what to spend, what not to spend, how to save, or where to invest or save.

No one has found a one-size-fits-all solution, and we don't expect anybody to, despite the various arguments and discussions around spending or saving money first (i.e., paying yourself first - as explored in Robert Kiyosaki's Rich Dad Poor Dad).

A mass technique would be an extraordinarily foolish way to advance, given the variance in salary levels, spending patterns, and basic requirements across the globe. What may work for one person may not work for another.

For this reason, I favor the concept of the Personal Spending and Earning Report (PSE), as it is presented at the very beginning of the book. The PSE helps you create your fiscal summary by taking into account your income, your expenses, your obligations that must be paid, and any other sporadic costs that are highly personal to you and, generally speaking, cannot be taken into account by any summarized planning application or format. This allows you to examine how you spend and save money, as well as how to make the most use of the money you now have or earn.

Generally speaking:

Spending is a particularly terrible habit that affects every financial decision you make since it determines how much money you have available. It has the power to truly ruin or make any plan or objective.

Starting With ThePse's Spending Section:

Transferring all the money you receive from your salary to an account offering higher interest should be your initial course of action. As an illustration, my salary account was with HDFC Bank while I worked at EY. They offered a 3.5% interest rate on savings accounts, but I could also get a 5.5% interest rate on all the money I deposited into my Kotak account. Although other banks offered greater profits as well, I chose to go with Kotak because it was a well-known and relatively more secure bank. This resulted in a 2% profit margin that was virtually risk-free from the entire money I did not spend from my pay. Additionally, using a single check card for purchases gives me a lot of reward points and cashback, which increases my profit margin from all of my spent funds by about 0.5% to 1%.

While I agree that following the Reserve Bank of India's (RBI) COVID-19 rate cuts, it has become a little problematic to see an open door in the larger banks, there are still many small money banks, such as Bandhan, AU Small Fin, and Jana Small Finance bank, that charge loan fees ranging from 5 to 6.75%. The large banks have examined their rates and reduced them to approximately 3%. Recently, the interchange has grown, but I have no idea how long it will endure.

Reaching the peril As a result of the recent failures of Yes Bank, PNB, and a number of other small banks, RBI requirements have tightened significantly. Therefore, we shouldn't be afraid of another bank failing. Therefore, I don't think this is a chance that one should give up on, even if we can constantly turn a few profit levels.

The second general guideline for spending is to make a plan and follow it while making purchases! The most frequent error we make is going over our monthly budget, which puts us in a position where we may have to rely on credit toward the end of the month to make ends meet. How can you now stay out of this predicament? The solution is as easy as improving discipline and planning. Make sure to budget your money for everything. This includes how much you spend on groceries, rent, utilities, phone bills, and other expenses. Additionally, ensure that your calculations are accurate and pertinent to your living level.

After everything is organized, total everything and include it in the PSE description in the book's presentation. It is now much easier to manage these than to deal with certain vulnerable sides that you thought may have existed or may have been completely missed. This will put all of your subsidizing holes, the remaining details, and the dark openings that suck your cash right before your eyes.

We classify all of the expenses into three main groups:

1. Needs: Expenditures necessary for endurance are referred to as essential spending. We all genuinely desire food, water, and a safe place to live, so this portion is natural. Additional essential expenses on your budget list may include medication, children's schooling, transportation/fuel charges, and training for yourself. This should undoubtedly constitute a sizable outlay, and your bank account should be enough to maintain you for three to six months necessities. People call it the stormy day reserve, although it's more of an asset for windy months. If something goes wrong, this asset will assist you in covering your expenses. I believe that people are intelligent enough to understand the meaning of it. Thus, I won't be going into greater detail.

2. Wants - Moving on to the supportive expenses, these various costs aren't truly necessary, but people can't live their lives without spending money in this area. I might want to include the amazing dress you saw online, a night of casual drinks, dinner with your significant other, and a quick getaway at the end of the week. These days, even though the great majority of us would agree that these matters are extremely important, a person cannot and should not consider these if they are just scraping by.

3. Desires: The extravagance head would include all the expenses you need to make but cannot due to your financial situation, such as buying that iPhone, going to an Upland Bistro that is well beyond your means, booking that five-star trip, etc. Additionally, you are aware of your deepest desires. You also recognize that you would have been free to spend that money had you not been in the current financial crisis.

Although it will fulfill you, this should be your least priority.

Returning to how you should spend, I would like to advise you that there is a very thin line separating the second and third types of expenses you incur. Continue to distinguish between comfort and extravagance, along with whatever works best for you. You must understand the difference, specifically, the financial difference that it would make to your PSE, continuously, consistently, and going forward, the impact on your overall way of life that you will make in five to ten years.

www.ingramcontent.com/pod-product-compliance
Lightning Source LLC
Chambersburg PA
CBHW071712210326
41597CB00017B/2445